EYEWITN
REVOLUTIONArT
PORTUGAL

EYEWITNESS IN REVOLUTIONARY PORTUGAL

Audrey Wise, MP

with a Preface by Judith Hart, MP

Spokesman Books
1975

Published by The Bertrand Russell Peace Foundation Ltd., Bertrand Russell
House, Gamble Street, Nottingham. NG7 4ET for *Spokesman Books*

Printed by
The Russell Press Ltd., Gamble Street Nottingham NG7 4ET.
Telephone: 0602 — 74505

CONTENTS

Introductory Note

Audrey Wise visited Portugal in the Summer of 1975, together with members of her family. She sought to find out about the effect of the Revolution on ordinary working people, and this little book reports her impressions and comments. Where she uses the word "we" Audrey Wise is referring to the family group with whom she was travelling.

Judith Hart's visit overlapped in time with that of Audrey Wise, and although both members of parliament naturally met and discussed what they had seen, each had different experiences to draw on. In addition to the preface which follows, it is hoped to publish a fuller account of Mrs Hart's impressions of revolutionary Portugal in the very near future.

Preface
Judith Hart, MP

The red carnations decorate tee-shirts and glasses. The posters proclaiming freedom and democracy and the power of the people are everywhere — beautiful, simple posters. Every wall in every village and town has its slogans and its competing array of party initials, and in Coimbra, towards the north, there are Chilean-style wall-paintings.

The streets of Lisbon are littered with leaflets advertising last night's demo, even as the early evening brings forth its small groups walking down the *Avenida da Liberdad* with their rolled banners, on their way to Rossio Square or Commercial Square for tonight's rally.

By late night, the cafes in the small towns north of Lisbon have their gathering of serious workers, intent on the television reports of what Cunhal has jut said, or Soares has said, or Copcon has said, impatient with chatterers, pleased to see foreign visitors so interested.

The place is alive with politics. There may, somewhere, be a silent majority who are either passive or bored, but we met no one without a view — from the harpist in the Conservatoire to the local bank manager, from the small hotelkeeper in the mountains (he was a fascist) to the building workers at the house we rent who talk politics all through their lunchbreak.

After 50 years of fascism, freedom is bursting out all over. It is not always entirely convenient for political parties structured on the conventional Western European hierarchical model, and, no doubt, a problem for the Armed Forces Movement Government. The tensions and disarray at the top, as Lisbon statements are issued and rejected, and the formal dialectic presents a new situation with every morning's newspapers, have perhaps themselves produced the impatient initiatives at the grassroots – the takeover of a factory, or a rural estate, by local workers' committee, then formalised after the event by the Government.

But after all, the programmes of all the parties of the Left which gained a precarious 51 per cent of the votes in the elections of last March for a constitutional assembly, with outright fascist parties banned, (note, by the way, that the elections were indeed for this purpose: not to elect a government, but an assembly to work out a new constitution to provide for an elected government) shared a strong socialist intent.

The most radical, indeed, was the programme shaped by the Congress of the Socialist Party: nationalisation, agrarian reform, workers' democracy, co-operatives, non-alignment. It is a programme which won the party its 38 per cent victory.

So the slogans which say "*Abaixo* (down with) *capitalismo e fascismo*" have got the mood right. For the Portuguese working class, after 50 years of what socialists, dissident socialists and communists alike described to us as "depoliticisation", may not have had time yet – in 16 months – to work out sophisticated plans within their party structures, but they have an understanding, innocent of compromise and expediency, of the relationship between the fascism which oppressed them, imprisoned them, tortured them, and sent their sons off to the last colonial wars, and the capitalism it protected.

Indeed, the real struggle in Portugal is not to be understood in terms of the conspiratorial theory of history. The Portuguese Communist Party has, of course, an influence and a power which goes well beyond its 12 to 13 per cent vote, partly because the MDP-CDE parties have a strength in some districts which gives important support to it. (In the main bank of one country town north of Lisbon, for example, 60 employees voted Communist or MDP in the March election, and 80 spread their votes over all the other parties).

It has key figures at the top — with Goncalves at the centre of current events. It seems not yet to have decided what kind of Communist Party it really is: but I think it likely that it will be neither Moscow, Chinese nor Cuban, but Portuguese communism. What is absolutely clear is that it wants a French-style co-operation with the socialists and other parties of the Left, excluding the ultra-Left Maoist groups.

The accepted British press version of events has it that it is the PCP which threatens a return to totalitarianism . If only the British press would get out of Lisbon and up to the north — as *The Observer* correspondent has done — they might see what is really happening, instead of sending back blinkered pieces which do not connect with reality, but which support the fevered efforts of international capitalism to protect its financial interests in Portugal.

And those newspapers which seem to be unduly angry with me at present might perhaps recall that two years ago one or two of us were right about Chile, and most of them were wrong; and that, with certain distinguished exceptions, they denied the truth about the tortures in Greece, so tragically substantiated in the Athens courtrooms this week.

And what is really happening is that there is frightening, if so far sporadic, violence against communists and other Left parties in the north; burnings of the northern countryside which go far beyond accident; the terrorisation of individuals; and press statements by Right-wing generals and commanders — including a Spinola interview with Associated Press in Brazil.

Chapter and verse? We saw the destruction and savage

havoc of stone-throwing and petrol-throwing in the PCP offices in Aveira, south of Oporto. We saw the preparations being made for defence against another attack, expected to follow a Right-wing demonstration that night in Aveira. I talked to a doctor who had been named in *Il Tempo*, an extreme Right journal, as a sinister communist. He was frightened: his car was parked well away from his home, and he was desperate to get home himself to his wife and children, "in case anything happened".

We saw the fires, and heard the stories, which *The Observer* also apparently heard, of the monoplane over the sea, supposedly from the Spanish fascists, whose slogans are here and there to be seen in the mountain villages near the Spanish border.

In the north, of course, are the naturally conservative peasant *minifundias*, in contrast to the agricultural labourers of the south. In the north is the strength of the Church, which in its social attitudes, is in sharp contrast to the Church in Chile. In the north, encouraged by conservatism, hatred of socialism whatever form it takes, and residual elements of fascism, the Right-wing elements in the MFA are vocal.

In such a situation, the talk is of the boycott of Portugal, of the leverage of the international financial world, of the economic problems which face its people, of the iniquities of the BBC Portuguese Service (whose main fault seems to be that it reports the British press), and of the failure of British understanding.

So there are things for us to do. There must be visits, and missions, and invitations. There must be built up a real understanding between ourselves and our socialist comrades in Portugal. There must be an appreciation of the challenge of charting a new democratic order on a blank sheet of paper, and, above all, real help wherever we can give it.

We offered it a few months ago, and a team from the

Ministry of Overseas Development went to Portugal in June. Now we must ask the Government to recognise that in the fragility of this Portuguese revolution, in their search for democracy and their determination to achieve a socialist society, and in their resistance to any new threat from the Right, the Portuguese people need our help.

My visit to Portugal

This visit to Portugal was under nobody's auspices but our own, paid for personally, and handled independently, seeking contact with as many different facets of what was happening in Portugal as possible, and people of differing views.

We were enormously helped by some members of the Transport & General Workers' Union (International Branch) and of the Portuguese Workers' Co-ordinating Committee in London, and especially by Alvaro Miranda, Sacuntala Miranda, and Carmen Maybolin, who translated endlessly.

Portugal faces great danger from the right, and enormous economic problems. Its government is in many ways weak and there are many currents struggling for advantage. Yet the overwhelming impression we have gained is of people trying to build a new future and of an infant democracy struggling to be born.

Those who paint this complex situation in any simplistic way, such as for instance a confrontation between the Socialist Party and the Communist Party to which everything else is subordinate, miss completely the groundswell of popular power and direct democracy which is by far the most exciting and probably the most significant feature.

In addition, this is a Revolution in a European country which has been activated through Colonial Revolutions and in which disillusioned conscript soldiers play an enormous part. To those who, like myself, view anything military with suspicion and reserve, to say the least, it is greatly heartening to see armed forces turning against their allotted role and playing quite a different part.

It is not true that there is repression and dictatorship in Portugal. In August 1975 the overwhelming atmosphere is one of free and intense discussion, delightful to be part of, and giving memories to treasure.

There are dark things happening as well, reactionaries setting fire to forests to cause as much damage as possible, and it doesn't take many of them to do this, especially if they can fly an aeroplane − probably from Spain − and drop some incendiaries on trees dry as tinder.

But there is far less violence in Portugal this August than there is in Britain. And we should remember this with all humility. Portugal's Revolution is a continuing process and it has been almost bloodless so far. It will stay this way if the Portuguese people are given even half a chance by the rest of the world.

Farmworkers in control

We visited a mixed farm of 1,400 hectares, which had been taken over by its workers on 14th July 1975. It was in the Beja district, about 120 miles south east of Lisbon, in the Alentejo province. The Alentejo is the main agricultural area of Portugal other than the wine-growing districts.

The vast majority of its workers are wage earners, agricultural workers in our sense rather than peasants. The farms are quite small, but one owner will possess many farms, so it is an area of small farms but large landowners.

The workers here have been very oppressed, and the situation is illustrated by the story of a woman who has become a heroine of the Alentejo. She was a leader of a strike for an 8-hour day, in the early 1960s. The National Republican Guard was sent out to deal with the strikers, and an officer asked her what she was doing and why they were not at work. When she answered that they were on strike for an 8-hour day, she was shot dead. She was pregnant at the time, and had a child with her.

Despite all this, the Alentejo had been a province whose people stayed put – it did not produce wanderers or migrants to cities. However, this changed with the colonial wars and many young people left not only their district but the country itself in order to escape being conscripted for four years. They also left to escape the high unemployment. So now there is a lack of young people in the Alentejo province.

In accordance with the usual pattern, the owner of the farm we visited has many other places, but this is the only one which has been occupied so far.

It is very much a mixed farm, growing some wheat, oats, maize and sunflowers. It carries about 100 cattle, 300 sheep and 100 pigs. There are about 3000 olive trees and some cork trees. Its main equipment is 3 tractors (we saw one of them, a Massey-Ferguson).

Before the Revolution 18 people were employed here but now there are 25, 23 men and 2 women.

This discussion took place in a cattle shed where there were about 3 dozen bullocks. We talked to at least 14 of the workers at considerable length.

Before the Revolution of 25th April, wages for the men here were 80 to 90 escudos per day (£1.50). After the Revolution but before the occupation wages, in common with all others in Portugal, had been increased substantially. Tractor drivers earned 190 escudos per day (£3.40), and the lowest male wage had reached 120 escudos per day (£2.16). Women earned 60 escudos per day (£1.08). The workers wanted all the men brought to 190, and the women to 120, and made a wage claim accordingly.

This claim meant no increase for the tractor drivers, who therefore did not support it, but they subsequently supported the occupation. Since the occupation the women's wages have been doubled, to 120 escudos per day and all the men now earn 160. This has meant an increase for all the men except the tractor drivers, who took a cut!

The farm's income is very seasonal rather than regular (the cattle are not dairy cows but are fattened for beef), so the workers are now being financed for the moment by the agricultural workers' union.

The workers are now substantially better paid than they were before the Revolution, but we asked them whether this was a real gain in view of increased prices.

They said they definitely were better off, but more important they felt more secure.

They also told us they get 75% of their wages as sick pay, and have had this since 1972/3 when it was granted as a result of a lot of unrest. However, in 1972/3 the wages were so low that 75% still left them in a desperate position. Now that wages have increased so much, they feel that this benefit is really worth something.

Since the occupation there are also various fringe benefits like use of the melons grown on the farm. Pursuing this line of fringe benefits, we asked if they would also now have free milk for their own use, but they were very surprised at the suggestion and we learned that in the Alentejo, milk is simply not regarded as a possible item of diet by farm workers, even for their chidlren. This is not due to any religious or sociological objection, but simply to the fact that it has always been far be-beyond them in price. So far beyond them that they did not even think of it as a luxury food for an occasional treat! It was not on their horizon at all.

Meeting agricultural workers who can never afford to drink milk is rather like imagining miners who could never have any coal. Note incidentally, they were all extremely small and thin.

We discussed their other living conditions. They mostly live in a group of houses tied to the farm, rent free but without electricity or other amenities. For example, one man said that for the past 14 years the five people in his family had lived in one room divided by a cloth.

The landowner has a house on this farm, and we asked why they had not taken this over and occupied it as well. They said it was because his furniture was still there. They want him to take his furniture away. They say they do not want his luxurious things, and that it would probably cause splits between them in any case. They repeated that they want better conditions than they have had, but not luxury, just simple things.

It was easy to see there had been plenty cause for discontent, but not so easy to understand what had triggered off the occupation of this particular farm (the first in the immediate vicinity) and the workers themselves did not seem too clear about it, though they were clearly proud of being the first in the neighbourhood.

The workers here do not consider that 1,400 hectares is big enough to be a satisfactory single unit and they are hoping there will be occupations nearby so they can form a co-operative. They think 2,000 hectares is the minimum necessary in this area, and they have had some contact with workers on nearby farms to try and encourage them to take over.

The wage claim had played a big part in stirring them up, but it clearly was not the only factor since some of the workers actually accepted a cut and only the women received the full amount of the claim.

The workers said that such a thing as taking over the farm would never have crossed their minds before 25th April.

We discussed how they worked the farm, and they told us they meet every Friday to discuss the week's happenings and to plan and distribute the work for the following week.

The overseer did not support the occupation and left the farm, but they are managing very well without him.

All the men attend the meetings, but not the women. They explained this by saying that "the women are wives", and that their work is "help" rather than "work". However, the women are full members of the agricultural workers' union (though they pay lower dues), and the men said the women could attend the meetings if they wanted to. It is interesting that despite the description of "help" and the non-attendance at the weekly meetings, the women nevertheless had had their wages doubled.

They said that the farm had been very much under-used and could produce a lot more. We asked whether it needed harder work or more equipment. They thought probably both, but said they would not mind the work because they now felt so much more interest in the farm and could work better. They now worked willingly whereas before they needed a lot of supervision. In many ways things are the same as usual, for instance they work the same hours, but they clearly felt very differently about their relationship to the work.

Before the Revolution there was a lot of unemployment, but this is being reduced. For example, six or seven additional workers have been on this farm since May 1975, placed there by the Union. This is part of the efforts being made to get the land more fully used, and to absorb more workers.

Employers must now notify the Union of all farm vacancies — this is not a legal requirement but nevertheless ways are found to ensure that it happens. The Union then fills the vacancies. Employers do not themselves choose which individuals they will take on.

All workers on this farm are members of the Union, and they told us that practically all workers in the Alentejo are Union members. The Union is still organised on a district basis, not nationally, and this particular district of Beja has one of the best Unions.

It had been organised straight after April 1974, and these workers had joined in June 1974. They had elected a shop steward and developed contact with the Union.

However, they told us they had not discussed the occupation with the Union first. They had decided for themselves and then informed it.

Since then they have had close contact with the Union, several times a week. The Union arranges advice on technical matters and, for example, the day before our visit an agricultural machinery technician had been there. He had decided they needed another tractor, and this would be provided free. (As a Coventry M.P., I hope it will be another Massey Ferguson.) Finance is being provided by the Government agency which has been set up for the reconstruction of agriculture, and which is co-operating with the Union. The Union has also opened a workshop for the repair of tractors, also free, and free fuel for the machines is being provided. The Union also requisitions privately owned tractors if they are not being used.

We asked these workers about their feelings on the Revolution, and what was the main benefit they felt since April 1974. They were quite adamant that the main benefit is a feeling of freedom and participation. Despite their poverty, they said this has meant even more than the money to them. They said they now feel able to work things out for themselves.

We asked whether they discussed politics much amongst themselves. They took this to mean party politics, and said No they did not think they knew much about this and they were really more interested in talking about the things which affected their daily lives and which they knew about.

However, when we asked them what they would think if there was a new government which wanted to give the farm back to the owner, they exploded into life, all declaring with the utmost vigour that it must never happen.

"We will fight. We will fight to the end — we will never give it back."

"This landowner here, he would not even open a well for us to drink from when we worked in the fields. We will never give it back."

*   *   *   *

We discussed the factual background of farm occupations with an official of the Ministry of Agriculture whose job at the moment is to go round the farms surveying the situation. He told us there is an Agrarian Reform law which provides for expropriation of farms of over 700 hectares by the State if there has been sabotage or the land is under-used. In addition, co-operatives are being encouraged, and occupations by workers will be legalised in the same circumstances.

These criteria seem to cover a great many of the farms, and occupations are proceeding apace. At the 21st August there were 55 ocupations in the district of Beja. The average size of the individual farm unit was 900 hectares and he reckoned that now about 50,000 hectares had been taken over by workers. This meant that about one third of the agrarian reform had now been carried out in Beja by means of workers' occupations.

This has reached a considerably higher proportion in the neighbouring district of Evora, where 100 farms had been occupied.

A neighbourhood assembly at work

"Inhabitants' Committees", which we would probably call Neighbourhood Committees if we had them, are springing up all over.

We saw a meeting announced at Palmela which is a village about 20 miles south of Lisbon, and went along to it. We asked permission to listen to the meeting and this was readily given.

The meeting was held in a place used as a semi open-air cinema. There were light-weight walls, and a metal framework roof covered with thickly growing plants, the framework being used to support lighting. About 200 people were present, probably a quarter of them women.

The meeting had started when we arrived, but was still on the Chairman's remarks. He was laying great stress on the need for people to talk freely and say what was in their minds.

A neighbourhood committee had sprung up and been in operation for some weeks, and this meeting was an attempt to broaden and formalise it.

The Chairman emphasised that everybody in the village had had the opportunity to come, and he again stressed the need for people to say what they really meant, and to help to solve the problems of the neighbourhood.

The Armed Forces Movement (MFA) is deeply involved in these attempts to build direct democracy or "popular power". Its General Assembly carried a decision in its favour on 8th July, and it was this which really sparked off the alarm of the right wing in Portugal.

Nothing is more dangerous to the right wing than people asserting themselves and attempting to come to their own decisions, and MFA commitment to direct democracy was of tremendous importance.

Indeed, we had also learned that the MFA is attempting to build democratic structures within the Armed Forces themselves.

I was therefore particularly interested in the contribution made by an MFA man at this village meeting, and I took a number of direct quotations from his speech. He said:

"Is it not the workers who create the wealth of a country? When the workers have control of the wealth they produce then we will have the Socialist Revolution.

"People's power is democracy for all those who have nothing, and have everything to gain. The right to health, the right to housing, the right to education.

"It is not enough to elect the neighbourhood committee and think they will solve the problems for you. It is necessary for people themselves to co-operate in solving problems.

"The functions of Workers' Committees and Neighbourhood Committees are complimentary.

"People must not think in terms of each one for himself but must think collectively for the benefit of the group. Each one for himself is a relic of the dark 50 years of fascism.

"The attacks on political party headquarters that we have witnessed are attempts by reaction to defeat the working class. When the people are not united then they will lose, and if we lose what we have won and what we expect to win soon, then we will lose a great deal."

He talked a little about Chile, then went back to Portugal.

"Fascism was the exploitation of workers on behalf of a small minority who just sunned themselves on the beaches. The highest of exploitation was the colonial war and the killing of the African people. Who made gains from the colonial wars? Only capitalists did — whilst we the people have 20,000 invalids as a result.

"What is happening in the North where the capitalists have

resorted to armed attacks can only be opposed by the people.

"We are expecting something to happen soon that may be like the 28th September or 11th March. (attempted counter coups). It is possible that this may be a more complicated problem. We hope this will not be so."

Then he talked about 25th April. We said the unity of the army and people was very important and it was the people who pushed the military forward and brought the revolution to where it is today.

"I would like to remind you that the objective of the reaction is to organise a fascist coup. Those people who have been connected with fascism, the PIDE (Secret Police), the reactionaries, at this moment have as an objective the creation of the necessary social base from which to carry out this coup. They are seeking division in the people, and the MFA, and are dividing the people of the North. The people of the North are not reactionary but are badly informed because the fascist reactionaries and the right wing political organisations have given wrong information and got them to be scared of communism. Reaction is now attempting to come down to the South of the country. We must be ready to remove the reactionary forces from our country."

There were other speeches from existing committee members. Things were clearly too left wing for one man in the audience, who stood up waving his arms and protesting loudly. Other people in turn leapt to their feet shouting at him with cries of "Reactionary". There was quite a commotion for a minute or two.

Then a woman went to the front of the meeting, and said she had something to say. She was handed the microphone and said:

"I would like to make an observation. People have been called here to discuss many problems. I came with maximum interest to follow a certain agenda." (The agenda contained 18 items.)

"There are things which must be dealt with objectively and calmly. In a small village like ours we must not get excited."

To the Chairman she said:

"You said at the beginning that people had the right to come here with all freedom and all sincerity. It is very important that we understand the problems of the Revolution and the position in relation to the MFA, but on the other hand there are also other problems which we need to discuss. We were told the meeting should finish at midnight and it is now 11pm, but we are still on the first part of the agenda. We have problems of flies etc. There are some points which are more important than ours and we have been hearing about them, but these other problems are also important to us. I apologise but I must insist. I think you have gone on too long, and this leads to confusion. I am sorry. I apologise, but it is my duty to say this."

The Chairman then said:

"I must criticise myself. The lady is quite right. I made a mistake. We will go on to the second point on the agenda. There is a proposal for the stepping down of some members of the committee."

The meeting was now very calm, but soon erupted into controversy of a different kind. There was a proposal that a certain person should withdraw from the committee because of a "moral problem". This caused a stir, and proved to be a very delicate matter indeed, but it was felt by the majority that the man had behaved badly and should not be on the committee.

Then the Chairman complained that some members of the committee did not attend, or arrived late and then wanted to leave at 11 pm.

It was proposed that one member withdraw for lack of attendance but he defended himself with great vigour and much arm-waving. He said he was a poor man and had animals to feed night and morning, and if he did not feed them he would not be able to feed his family. He had no one to help him and it was necessary for a poor man to work. If the meetings got on with things more quickly they would take less time and it would be easier for him. No one should say he was a bad man – he was a good man – a friend to all the men in the village, and a friend to all the women!

At this, the meeting dissolved into uncontrolled hilarity. However, his defence won the day and he was voted back on to the committee.

Another man said he had had disagreement with some of the policies of the committee but he was willing to have another try if the meeting felt he should do so. He also was voted back on. Some additional people were elected. Then the Chairman said:

"We have no women. We must have some women. Many of the things we are talking about are of great importance to women and they should be there."

He asked for volunteers. Four women stood up and were voted on, but only three were elected. One was clearly not at all popular, and there were mutterings from people near us, saying "She doesn't look after her children properly", and she failed to get elected. However, this was not opposition to her simply because she had children, as two of the women who were elected actually had babies in their arms, and they were elected without any difficulty. It was very clearly the first time women had played such parts.

They then moved to Item 3 — the Children's Park. This was something which was in the course of being made, and some play equipment had now been obtained. The meeting decided it would be best to finish it themselves with volunteers for building a wall, levelling some ground, and so on. The Chairman said they would need lorries, equipment for levelling and volunteers for the actual work.

While this item was being discussed, a woman sitting near us was quietly grumbling to herself and her neighbours. She was saying: "We need nurseries more than a park so that we can work to earn some money." The man next to her was reproachful. "Shouldn't the children have somewhere to play?" he asked. "Yes," said the woman, "but I have to work 9 hours a day to help keep

my family and I have no one to look after my little
ones. I have to pay many escudos every day to have
them looked after – nearly as much as I earn."

She got quite heated about this but not brave enough
to go to the front to say it. In the meantime, the children's park item proceeded.

Then they moved to the "Vaccination Centre". Our
neighbour said, "That, yes, that I agree with. That is important." The Chairman said:

"We must prove we have a need for this. We intend to do a
survey and would like to appeal to people present to ask every-
one to come to us and tell us their health needs. We have a
garage we are going to use as an office, and will be there between 6.30 and 9.30 every night. Now that we have this big
meeting, it will be possible for us to know all the health
problems."

The meeting was now moving at a cracking pace, and
got on to housing problems. However, it was now midnight, and the Chairman asked whether the meeting
wanted to finish or continue. It opted to continue, and
went on to discuss lack of sanitation and bathrooms.

Some places did not have a sewer, and they wanted
this put right. In addition, there were problems between
landlords and tenants.

The thing which caused concern was not the
problems of large landlords, but those of the small landlord – not rich, but with steady enough work to have
bought say a single house to provide for his old age. The
committee had been struck with the difficulty of decid-
ing where the greatest injustice lay: with the tenant who
had no bathroom or with this small landlord who could
not face the financial burden of providing one. They
were very anxious to be fair to both sides.

It was decided that the committee should try to draw
up some guide lines about this, and that perhaps some
other way might have to be found so that bathrooms
could be provided.

It was also pointed out that where landlords simply refuse to provide bathrooms, there is power now for these to be installed and the cost deducted from the rent.

The committee would produce a form on which people could say what attempts had been made with the landlord to get a bathroom. When there were problems between landlord and tenant, the committee would have to work out what to do for the best.

We reluctantly left at this stage of the meeting as it was now 12.15 am and we were leaving early next morning to visit the north.

The meeting had been a fascinating experience. The high points were: some of the remarks of the MFA soldier, especially those about the colonial wars, and about the workers being creators of the wealth; the stress laid on freedom of expression, and the willingness with which this was pursued, including the controversies and the criticisms expressed of the meeting itself; being in a situation where reform and revolution were not alternatives but were actually part of the same process.

Democracy was struggling into being in this village, and it was a rare treat to be able to witness it.

Workers' control at the brewery (a visit to SCC)

SCC is the Portuguese brewing concern, which belongs to one of the largest financial groups in Portugal.

We spent a whole day and a half in detailed discussion with high officials including civilian and military members of the Government-appointed Commission of Administration (equivalent to a Board of Directors) at its Lisbon headquarters, and members of the Workers' Committee at the main brewery about 20 miles northwest of Lisbon.

The group brews beer, and more recently has produced Schweppes and other drinks under licence. It makes glasses, grows hops, and has various other diverse interests. It is also very important in the Portuguese colonies and in Brazil. It started in 1934 and later there were substantial take-overs, in 1947 particularly.

It has made large profits, and its workers are something of an aristocracy of labour, having some of the most advanced working conditions and wages in Portugal. Unusually for Portugal, the company tended to use higher wages rather than repression in order to avoid problems, and when the national minimum wages were 3,000 escudos per month, wages here were 6,000 (£55.50).

We heard something of its financial history. The initial capital in 1934 was 100,000 escudos. Repeated bonus issues to existing shareholders, however, brought share capital to 300 *million* escudos by 1973.

In 1973 they issued further shares for public subscription. Workers and the public subscribed 250m escudos, and the old Director/shareholders subscribed 150m, but still the old Director/shareholders held the vast majority of the capital, because of the previous bonus issues.

1,000 million escudos had been issued as dividends between 1934 and 1974.

Workers' Take-Over and Inquiry

In January 1975, there was a big meeting about wages etc. When the Directors first arrived they were applauded. However, the meeting lasted several days and certain things started to come to light.

The feeling of the workers changed, and they took advantage of the Annual Dinner of the Directors in order to take the place over.

The original problem at the meeting concerned different payments for workers who considered they were doing similar jobs. For instance, one group was given a higher wage, back-dated for 12 months, whereas other workers got much less for the same job. This tactic was intended to divide the workers, but in fact it triggered off the close-down of the factory by the workers and led to the further developments.

Thirty demands were formulated and put to the Directors, and all but thirteen were agreed. The main clause with which the Directors did not agree was the reduction of their own salaries.

The Directors were paying themselves 70,000 escudos per month (about £1250), plus share dividends. There were 13 of them, and the workers also demanded that their number be reduced to five.

They also had massive perks such as free petrol, free fuel for home central heating, 100,00 escudos a year for buying a car, and their car repairs paid for.

This kind of thing was common in Portuguese management. When the workers closed the factory they set up an Inquiry Committee to look into these things in the whole financial group.

The Inquiry Committee began operations on 20th February and finished at the end of July, having issued a report. We saw some of its very detailed and complex results, outlining the whole financial structure.

The reason why the Inquiry was so successful in obtaining a mass of information was that it was completely unexpected, and so the documents were still available. Other companies and banks have learnt the lesson and removed such documents.

The Inquiry Committee found that between 1965-74 the company had paid to the Director/shareholders 450 million escudos in dividends, salaries and perks, and also paid personal taxes, and "confidential expenses".

It has lent to other companies in the group, mostly interest-free, 310m escudos. This company, S.C.C., was used as the banking company of the group. They invested in buying other enterprises, associated companies, often valueless, and expended 350m escudos on this. At the end of 1974 they had a debt of 1,000m escudos of which 900m was owed to one bank which was also a shareholder.

The company did not pay its taxes. It simply did not set money aside for tax payment and just did not pay — no sophisticated avoidance or even evasion. Nevertheless no action whatever was taken. This appears to have been common, but people did not know. The newspapers were mostly owned by the banks anyway.

The company also distributed non-existent profits as dividends and at the end of 1974 a large amount of a loan was paid out in dividends.

The Director/shareholders often acted illegally. More than 100m escudos were transferred illegally to Brazil. A phantom company called Vita-Finance was set up in Panama in order to control the investment in Brazil. The money put in was 200m escudos but the company was valued at 400m escudos. 150m escudos were transferred to Angola illegally.

The company also indulged in price manipulation between its sections in Portugal and abroad. It over-priced or under-priced its transactions between subsidiaries at will. Such transfer pricing is common with the growth of multi-nationals, and needs investigating in Britain also.

In contrast with Britain, Portuguese finance and industrial capital are completely fused. There is also less foreign capital because Salazar originally had laws to control foreign investment, as the aim was to build a national fascist capitalism. The law was changed in 1965 and foreign capital started to flood in.

The colonial wars had curious effects on the economy of Portugal and the colonies. They meant that soldiers and often their families were in the colonies and there was therefore an increased market. Also, groups of negroes were paid high wages. They did not change their style of living as regards housing etc., often living in very poor conditions indeed, but nevertheless they bought consumer goods. This was in addition to the distorting effect already caused through the imposition of quota systems on the colonies which compelled them to take Portuguese exports.

So the Portuguese economy became very dependent on its colonies, as well as being financially drained by the wars needed to retain them.

Even before 11th March, the workers' Inquiry Committee had in its hands more than enough information to have the Directors arrested for fraud, but this was not done. They met the Economics Minister (a Socialist Party member), but he said "This was normal practice" and declined to do anything. After 11th March, the Directors disappeared.

Nationalisation

Before the 11th March, as they discovered how the company had been run, the workers became very dissatisfied and asked the Government to take it over. However, at that stage there had been no new nationalisation.

Of course, there had been nationalisation under fascism, which illustrates that nationalisation need by no means be a socialist measure. It depends on the purposes and the methods used.

It is important to realise that the Revolution has passed through different stages since 25th April 1974. Before 11th March 1975, the policy of the first and second governments had really been to defend capitalism in general, improve it and make it work without fascism, and if necessary defend it against individual capitalists. So the government had taken the power to take over companies in order to avoid the flight of capital and economic sabotage, but only after the company directors left.

So when the workers first asked the government to take over, this was not at first responded to.

After 11th March and the failure of the attempted coup by Spinola in conjunction with the right wing, there was the third government and it took a left turn and there was talk of "socialising".

After the Directors fled, the Government appointed a Commission of Administration (Board of Directors) of five people. This consisted of three people nominated by the Inquiry Committee. The workers accepted these nominees, but do not regard them as direct workers' representatives as they did not consider they were yet in a position to be directly represented, nor was the company actually nationalised. Then there were two other members directly appointed by the Government, one a civilian who had been with British Leyland, and the other a Navy commander from the MFA. We talked at length separately with these two Government appointees.

About a week before our visit, the company had been

nationalised. This was the first action of the fifth government, but had already been prepared by the fourth government. As well as the brewery, nationalisation covered shipyards, and the CUF which is the largest group in Portugal, very early established and traditional, resistant until recently to foreign capital. CUF owns about 10% of Portuguese industrial capacity.

Practically all the big groups are now nationalised, covering more than 75% of Portuguese manufacturing.

The second largest group in Portugal is the Champalimaud group, which is younger, more modern, aggressive, tied to foreign capital, able to compete internationally. It is a focus for multi-national development and had close connections with Spinola. Champalimaud himself is now in Brazil, trying to take over group assets there.

There has been no nationalisation of foreign capital yet, so the situation is rather confused. It may be that there will be some reciprocal ownership recognition, especially with Brazil so that Portugal takes over Brazilian assets in Portugal and Brazil takes Portuguese assets in Brazil.

Compensation has not yet been paid, but the nationalisation law says that the question of compensation will be "studied".

The opinion was expressed to us most strongly that for example in the case of S.C.C. it would probably be decided that the ex-owners had already received their compensation in advance, as it were, through their previous milking.

Textiles and electronics have not been nationalised. They are multi-national controlled and very much geared to low wages. In some cases they are now leaving the country, since low wages will no longer be tolerated. Tourism is also outside nationalisation so far, though we heard of some worker take-overs.

The situation regarding foreign capital is very confused. For example, IMA is partly owned by British Leyland and assembles lorries etc. Another concern is an agency, Portuguese owned, for assembly of CKD stuff. This is typical. There is considerable sub-contract work, and sections of Portuguese industry are heavily dependent on foreign technology and a great deal is paid out for licences.

A good many difficulties are being placed in the path of Portuguese companies now. We were told of difficulties being created for S.C.C. by international capitalism. For example, the previous Directors had negotiated a loan of 4 million dollars from the First National City Bank of New York. When those Directors lost control, the bank refused to proceed with the loan. They have made several attempts to get the usual loans which the company used to get without any trouble, but they cannot even get replies.

Another similar case is that of SECIL which is a cement company, part Danish capital, which had negotiated a loan of 18 million dollars which has also not been proceeded with.

As in many other cases, S.C.C. needs certain foreign supplies and foreign equipment, but the supply contracts for these have been unilaterally cancelled and foreign sellers are now selling against immediate money only. Since nationalisation, letters of credit issued by Portuguese banks are not being accepted, only those issued by foreign banks.

Before they were nationalised, Portuguese banks themselves were manipulating the payments made by Portuguese emigrants, which normally covered the balance of trade deficit, so that the foreign currency never actually came in. Money was transferred horizontally from the emigrants' accounts abroad to accounts opened by wealthy Portuguese, in the foreign branches, and from the accounts of the wealthy Portuguese were getting foreign currency into their accounts abroad, the emigrants' home accounts were being credited with their remittances, but no foreign currency was actually coming in.

We were also informed that export orders are being cancelled, especially in the metal industries.

Now that S.C.C. has been nationalised, the interim Commission of Administration will be replaced. The normal pattern in nationalised enterprises is for there to be a Commission of Administration of three members, one of whom is nominated by the workers, and two by the government but the government nominees are subject to workers' veto.

So far, in S.C.C. it appears that the Workers' Committees in the various parts of the enterprise have not been able to reach agreement on one nominee or direct appointment by them. They have therefore decided to put forward seven nominees and ask the government to make the final choice. As the whole structure is so new and the component parts of the enterprise are in several different areas, it will clearly take time to build up cohesion between the various Workers' Committees.

So far, workers' control has remained at production level. There is a division between administration and general policy on the one hand, and the conduct of production on the other. The Workers' Committee can make recommendations to the Commission of Administration and it is discussing the extension of workers' control from production to broader policy aspects. In practice, decisions by the Commission of Administration are now not taken without meeting Workers' Committees.

There are Workers' Committees in each component part, factories, warehouses, offices.

Payment for members of the Commission of Administration has been fixed by the Government at 30,000 escudos per month gross (£545) which amounts to about 20,000 nett (£363). In S.C.C. the average monthly remuneration of employees is about 8,000 escudos nett

(£145). The S.C.C. minimum is 6,000 gross, about 5,600 nett (£100).

Relationship with the Armed Forces Movement

We asked the Armed Forces Movement member how he was chosen for this job. He told us that the workers in the course of their mass meetings in January had asked the local MFA to send a representative. He is a Naval commander in Lisbon and was given this task.

He then acted as intermediary between the workers and the Supreme Revolutionary Council and the Government, when the workers were in conflict with the old Board of Directors.

When the interim Commission of Administration was set up by the government to replace the previous Board of Directors after 11th March, the Government chose him as the military member because he was already familiar with the problems and had the confidence of the workers. He is not directly an MFA representative and does not report to them as such.

We asked him how he saw his particular role. He said that his job was to apply the programme of the MFA in relation to this company, especially insofar as this involves favouring the oppressed classes.

He said there were difficulties in this company because the majority of the workers here he termed petit bourgeois in the sense that their wages are much higher than normal. The gross national product per month divided by head of population gives a figure of 3,000 escudos. The Government has fixed a minimum national male wage of 4,000 escudos per month except for agricultural workers and domestic employees. The S.C.C. minimum is 6,000 escudos per month.

He said it has been difficult to obtain a feeling of solidarity. This particular company had previously used higher wages to buy off trouble rather than be as oppressive as other Portuguese employers.

Following 25th April, they put up wages again in May 1974, before the Government's instruction, perhaps in order to head off any revolutionary fervour. The workers continued to see their wage demands very much in terms of differentials, and so wage demands in certain sectors continue to the possible detriment of less well paid workers.

We asked about other kinds of benefits, and he explained that the workers at S.C.C. have free transport to factories, pay 5 escudos for meals compared to the real cost of 50 escudos, and there are other fringe benefits such as maternity benefits.

We asked whether workers' control of the division of remuneration — that is allowing the workers themselves to allocate the remuneration for different groups of workers from the total amount available — had been considered. He said that they had not thought of doing this, but the workers' committees themselves are considering all aspects of workers' control.

He said that as yet on wages workers see the problem in terms of their own functions rather than collectively. They are thinking of initiating "pluri-activity", that is, changes of jobs so that people see each other's problems instead of doing always one job only and seeing just their own problems, but they have not started this yet.

We asked about the level of interest shown by the workers. He said that of course some workers were not interested in control at all. Some whom he termed social democrats want control of the enterprise strictly for the benefit of its own workers, others whom he termed socialists want control of the enterprise for the benefit of the working class as a whole.

He is personally very interested in an alliance between the MFA and the Workers' Committees. There are no workers' committees in the armed forces yet. They are in the process of transition, so that not only officers will be sent as representatives to workers' committees.

We have learnt that the sovereign power in the MFA is the General Assembly, which has elected members. All military units are represented in the General Assembly of the Armed Forces Movement.

In the navy, democracy is being started by means of "wellbeing" committees (something like a welfare committee). Officers, sergeants and sailors are all represented proportionally, with the proviso that no one group can have an absolute majority. For example, there may well be three officers, four sergeants and seven sailors on a committee.

We asked about the new role of the armed forces, which after all have been one of the repressive arms of fascism for fifty years, and yet are now talking in terms of socialist revolution.

He said it was a paradox. But the armed forces of Portugal are conscript forces. Even the navy has been composed mainly of conscripts for at least the past 10 years. The need for people to fight in the colonial wars was so great that there was no alternative but to obtain them through conscription, and for four years. It was widely hated, and there were many young men who fled the country to escape the draft.

So the armed forces were largely composed of the sons of workers. Even before 25th April, there was much restlessness and worry in the armed forces about the colonial wars. Realisation was coming that they were being used against their own interests.

We saw a cartoon inside a bank window which portrayed this process. It showed workers clearly very overburdened and poor; it showed soldiers fighting Africans; and it showed other people who clearly were living in luxury on the backs of all these things. Then it showed soldiers gathering in groups and realisation dawning. It showed them turning on the rich and joining hands with the poor workers.

We have learnt that the relationship between the

General Assembly of the MFA and the Supreme Council of the Revolution is in principle that the Supreme Council should be elected by the General Assembly, but this is not yet done and the MFA is not yet fully democratic.

But on 8th July, the General Assembly took decisions in favour of Popular Assemblies, with direct links between the MFA, Workers' and Neighbourhood Committees. It was this decision which greatly alarmed the "moderates". It was the real trigger of the present crisis. It showed that Popular Power (perhaps more meaningfully expressed here as Direct Democracy) is a reality coming to life.

The Workers' Committee

The Workers' Committee is made up entirely of manual workers. The only real contact it has had with the clerical workers was during the "saneamento", the period of "cleansing" of fascists from positions of authority.

The reason there are no clerical workers on the Committee is that under the fascists there was a pseudo-Workers' Committee which was management appointed, from the clerical staff.

The restriction of the Workers' Committee to manual workers was approved by a mass meeting of all workers, including clerical. However, it has now been realised that manual workers alone cannot operate the factory, and it has now been agreed that a further four members be elected to the Workers' Committee, and that these four can be office workers.

There has been no compulsory "cleansing" by the Workers' Committee, but there has been "self-cleansing". For example, a high administrator has gone to Brazil on an extended holiday. Another has accepted a job in Spain! The Commission of Administration wanted to keep the man now in Spain, but the Committee said that there were only two positions: either you are or the

Revolution or against, and since the man was against, he had better stay in Spain.

All demands emanate from the workers at mass meetings. There are lots of problems raised, including wages. But conditions of work are their main preoccupation.

Although the offices for the management are luxurious, the conditions on the factory floor are poor. For instance, one section suffered from the extreme heat in the summer and from the cold in the winter. Methods are now being investigated to ensure an equable temperature at all times.

The Workers' Committee is very anxious to achieve full workers' control. They are looking for ideas on this, and would welcome printed material.

The Workers' Committee feels that it is most important to involve the maximum number of workers in the control, and towards this they have now formed Section Committees whose concern is with production, but they are still not satisfied with the number of workers involved. The Committee is now thinking of holding mass meetings every three months to discuss workers' control.

By workers' control, they do not mean about production methods only, but *what is being produced, why it should be produced, and for whom.*

They have already established some control on the buying of raw materials. They decide how much of various materials is required, for example the number of crates that will be needed to hold the bottles. They claim that under the previous management, there was very bad and inefficient buying. For example, thirty tonnes of glue had to be thrown away because it became useless; 28 tonnes of essence was ordered from Israel without first getting samples, and the essence was found to be useless. This, they said, could not happen under workers' control.

After the old Directors fled, the Committee found that the workers at a farm owned by the company had been left without any wages. There was fruit at the farm, so the Workers' Committee arranged to buy this fruit for their canteen and so the farmworkers got their wages.

When we were talking to the MFA member of the Commission of Administration earlier, we had asked whether they had developed any vertical links of this kind, going back to the raw material suppliers such as farm workers, in an attempt to build the solidarity he had been talking about. He said it was an interesting suggestion, but they had not tried it. We noticed that he was wrong on this, and that the Workers' Committee at the Brewery had in fact put it into practice, at least a little and established such a direct link.

They mentioned the royalties S.C.C. has to pay especially to Schweppes, for formulae used. These are very heavy, although all but two of the formulae concerned had been invented at S.C.C. We were told that attempts had been made to get Schweppes to stop these royalties, but that Schweppes had replied that the British Government had told them they had a legal entitlement and should continue to demand the royalties.

We discussed the thorny question of wage differentials. The former administration had divided the workers by wage differentials. For example, in an electrical setion which employed 23 workers there were 12 wage levels.

We put this question: "If the management said: 'Here is x amount of money to be shared out as wages', how would the Committee handle this?"

They said that if the amount of money was sufficient, they would close the factory down for the day and hold a mass meeting of all workers to decide how it should be shared.

We asked: "And if not sufficient?"

They said the Committee would point out that the government had frozen the company's assets but that extra money would have to be found for wages.

The Workers' Committee determines the employment of new labour, and at present they insist that only workers who are unemployed can be taken on.

The Workers' Committee controls the sacking of workers. For example, recently the management wanted to sack ten workers for absenteeism. The Committee looked into the matter and found that two of the workers had lost a lot of time. The Committee had a talk with this two, then told the management they could not sack them, but if in future they were absent for a certain period over a certain length of time, then the management could sack them without consulting the committee.

For the rest, the Committee found they had only lost a few days during the last six months, and would not agree to their being sacked. On the contrary, the Committee felt that the Personnel Officer who wanted to do the sacking should be sacked himself for wasting time!

The Workers' Committee were 100% in agreement with workers' control, and were trying to sort out what form this should take.

The Government had put in a Commission of Administration which at least was not against workers' control. If it had been, then its removal would have been demanded.

The Workers' Committee has fortnightly meetings with the Commission of Administration.

The people who are Government nominated for the Commission of Administration must have the confidence of the workers, or we were told they would not be accepted.

What happened at Republica

We visited *Republica* and talked at length with an office worker and a print worker. Before 25th April *Republica* was an independent "anti fascist" paper which means that it did not conform willingly but was frequently censored, and in the so-called 'election' times when censorship was briefly dispensed with, then *Republica* supported any opposition candidates. Its workers were fairly conscious already, and chose to work for *Republica* deliberately, even though for a long time its wage rates were very low, about 60% of average wages. This arose because before 1971 *Republica* had a very low circulation, between 5 and 7000 (except in so-called election periods).

However there was a law obliging newspapers to have a certain figure of capital; *Republica* did not fulfil this requirement and was going to be closed down. Additional shares were created and were bought by people who are now in the Socialist Party leadership. They had put in a new business Manager in 1969 and by 1971 the circulation started to increase. Immediately before April 1974 it had reached 45,000 to 50,000 and the workers' wages had increased to average levels. The workers felt that this was due largely to the efficiency of the new business manager. After 25th April, circulation increased to 60,000 to 70,000.

After 25th April, the majority of journalists emerged as members of sympathisers of the Communist Party (PCP) or the MDP, which is a party very close to the PCP. They balanced the Editor who favoured the

Socialist Party (PS). However at this time, the parties started to struggle to get control of daily newspapers and at *Republica* this took the form of a struggle between the majority of the journalists versus the editor and management (general manager and directors), PCP versus PS.

New journalists were taken on and given jobs of political commentary and writing in depth, whereas the existing journalists were relegated to minor jobs. Some drifted away.

At first the print workers stood aloof from this. They considered the established PCP journalists to be technically good (better than the new ones) but these journalists had themselves taken bad positions in relation to other press struggles, including one where the workers were trying to remove their fascist director. So the other workers at *Republica* were not inclined to support the PCP journalists in their own conflict with the PS editor. Having failed to gain the support of the other workers, 12 journalists left in March 1975. *Republica* then became virtually a PS paper. It was never, however, the party organ and the socialist party has in fact an official party paper. Its PS influence arose because its major shareholders were individual leaders of the PS, who had gained their interest in the paper from coming to its rescue and having the cash to do so.

The other workers, (printers, office workers, and others) then decided that they should not ignore the situation that had arisen. Not having wished to support PCP control did not mean that they favoured PS control. They wanted a broad paper, favourable to the working class, but giving various viewpoints.

So there was a meeting between workers and management, at which it was agreed that the paper should remain independent. The business manager supported the workers and worked out a plan of restructuring in order to guarantee the workers' demands. However, this plan was not carried out and the paper became more and more a vehicle for the PS alone with the front page dominated by PS statements every day, instead of carrying varying left wing viewpoints. The business manager became very dissatisfied and felt that he himself was now being squeezed out, therefore he threatened to leave on 15th May, 1975. He was told he was dismissed and this triggered off workers discussion, as a result of which the editor and directors were asked to come to a mass meeting but refused to do so.

The directors then wanted to put a statement about the internal problem of the paper on the front page, but the workers refused to print it. The directors then said the paper should not be published but as it was ready, the workers then brought it out themselves in its originally prepared form. About 45 minutes after the workers decided to print it themselves, there was a statement on the street, supposedly from 20,000 readers of the paper, saying that the journalists and editor were imprisoned in the offices. In fact they had been told they could leave but they would not be allowed back in, (though even this decision was subsequently relaxed). The editor spoke from the windows through a loud hailer and a loud speaker was touring Lisbon, claiming that the PCP had taken over.

It is important to realise that the total number of workers is 175 and of these only 24 opposed the action, (a telephonist, a photographer and 22 journalists). The remainder, including 6 journalists, support the action. The majority of the print workers were socialist party sympathisers or members originally. In fact the office worker who talked to us had started as a socialist party member.

These events took place on 15th May, but the claim that the PCP was taking over the paper had been foreshadowed earlier. On 2nd May, the paper had not been published and on 3rd May Mario Soares had claimed that the PCP was trying to take it over. On 4th May he had to apologise for this mis-statement. However this seems to indicate that the socialist party was expecting trouble and preparing to claim that the PCP was responsible. The workers are adamant that this is completely untrue.

The present position is that a set of editorial rules have been drawn up which make it clear that the paper is to be of the working class and for the working class. It is to be a newspaper whose task is above all to give news of struggles and it is now trying to forge links with workers' committees and neighbourhood committees. They are trying to find a new structure, different from an editor with complete control, and designed to give more weight to the views of the workers as a whole. The content is now being prepared by 7 journalists and 11 trainee journalists. It is intended to set up a committee with representatives from each section. The journalists will recommend content and lay out, which will then be approved by the workers' committee, not as to specific content but in order to see that the editorial rules are being carried out.

At the moment there is a workers' co-ordinating committee which at present is the organ through which ideas and anything in the life of the newspaper is channelled, though the final decision is taken by the workers as a whole at a mass meeting. The composition of the workers co-ordinating committee is; 4 print workers; 3 office workers; 2 from the dispatch dept.; 1 proof reader; 1 driver; and one press operator. There are no journalists as yet, because most of the journalists now working for the paper are new and it is felt that they should have more time to prove their support for the aims of the paper since they were not present during the struggle to keep it as a broad paper of the workers.

The ownership of the paper is still in its previous hands, that is the hands of Mario Soares and his friends, but not of the socialist party as such. These people are in *Republica* entirely as individuals.

Because the workers' co-ordinating committee insisted that the paper should resume publication, which it did on 8th July, the Government established a provisional administrative board, military in composition which negotiates with the workers co-ordinating committee. It comes to the premises but so far there has not been any dispute with the workers co-ordinating committee, and the paper is able to appear every day.

Republica is not in any way acting as a PCP organ. We ourselves had an opportunity to witness its methods, quite accidently. A *Republica* worker attended the village meeting at Palmela, described elsewhere in this booklet, and asked permission for photographs and a report to be made. He stated there that *Republica* regards the neighbourhood committees with the workers' committee as its natural correspondents, and we thus had evidence of the practical attempts being made to build up the relationship which had been mentioned to us when we had visited *Republica.* We came away feeling that we were seeing a quite proper expression of press freedom and that the action of the *Republica* workers in taking over the publication deserved support rather than criticism.

The Post Office workers' union

We had evidence of a great upsurge in trade union organisation and activity, and indeed there were many
union elections going on while we were in Portugal.

We talked with a member of the Executive, which
they call the National Secretariat, of the Post Office
Workers Union who gave us information about the Union.

It is of course, newly formed. There was for several
months a lot of activity by a preparatory committee
composed of people who were anxious to start a proper
trade union. It has a democratic structure and has now
reached 35,000 members. As we found in the case of
the agricultural workers in the Alantejo, all the workers
are anxious to join the union.

We asked what had been achieved so far. He said
there had been decasualisation of 5000 jobs, and also
the employment of regular relief workers on a proper
basis. They were achieving a feeling of unity between
different kinds and grades of workers. To help this, the
number of grades had been vastly reduced. Before, there
were 150 different grades including 6 grades of postmen,
now there were only 6 grades altogether.

They were also achieving equalisation between workers in Lisbon and outside. This particular member lived
in Evora, which is about 90 miles from Lisbon. He is a
sorter, and still works at the trade because the union has
no full time officials. It does not seem to be contem-
plating having full time officers, but it has three full
time office workers for the whole country and hopes to
increase these to 9 or 10.

We found this tendency for union officers to remain working at trade elsewhere also. For example, the President of the Textile Workers Union still works at the trade.

Both men and women are members of the Union.

There are 21 people on the National Secretariat including three women. Elections are by secret ballot. They are substantially different from any union elections we know of this in this country. There are alternative slates or lists of candidates who get together to stand as a unit on the basis of a particular programme. There is no limit on how many lists there can be, although we did observe in the various union elections taking place that it tends to resolve itself into "Lista A" and "Lista B". However there is no bar to additional lists going forward.

In the Post Office, workers' union elections will be every two years. Regional elections follow national elections within 30 days.

The list system means that the whole slate is elected or not elected en bloc. Because it is closely tied to the programme that the candidates all stand on it has the advantage of making it more likely that the people elected will actually carry out the programme whereas if policy decisions are quite separate from elections then it can and does happen that policies are not carried out. This is an advantage for the list system. However, the disadvantage seems to us to be that there will not at any given time be any minority expression on an executive. We think the main importance of this is that it makes it difficult for dissenters to obtain information about what is being done at the top. This seems to us to be a grave disadvantage of this list system. There is no special machinery for groups to come together to form lists. It is entirely up to those who wish to involve themselves.

In the Post Office elections there were two lists and we asked about the composition and programme. Of course, our information was coming from one of the victorious list. This broadly speaking was regarded as a list of the "revolutionary left", although six out of the 21 on the list did not belong to any party or group. The others belonged to five different groups or parties, including one member of the PCP. There were no members of the PS on the list. Its programme included demands for "Saneamento" of the Post Office. This was a term we came across a number of times, and can be translated as "clean up" or removal of fascists from positions of authority. It included demands relating to the supply of medicine which arose because Post Office workers in Lisbon had concessions for obtaining medicines, but this did not apply in the rest of the country. The demand was to make it country-wide. This had now been achieved.

The defeated list was entirely composed of PCP members or supporters. There was some overlap in the two programmes such as on the issue of the medicines, but we were told that the PCP list did not mention either wages or "Saneamento" (cleansing). It included the demand for the restructuring of the PO but did not give details.

Demonstrations and rallies

We were told about some demonstrations which had
taken place earlier, and we attended some ourselves.

The accounts of the earlier demonstrations were given
to us when we visited SCC (the brewery group). We confirmed some of the information from other sources also.

End August, 1974. The first demonstration to make
an impact was during the second government at the end
of August 1974, and was called by the Lagnave shipyard
workers against a law very like the Industrial Relations
Act (forbidding sympathy strikes etc.).

The shipyard workers, in their overalls and helmets,
made an impressive sight. They appealed to the soldiers,
who were brought into the streets to prevent the march,
over the heads of their officers, and they were allowed
to march. They made the law a dead letter.

The demonstration had also been backed by the Post
Office Workers. There had been two national strikes, by
the Post Office Workers and by the Textile Workers, and
both had been opposed by the Communist Party (PCP).
This was confirmed for me by an official of the Communist Party, who strongly defended this opposition.
We discussed in detail the Post Office situation, but he
failed to convince me that their opposition had been
justified.

On 24th January, 1975, there was a big demonstration in Lisbon to support the decision to have only one
Trade Union Confederation.

The Socialist Party (PS) had wanted a plurality of

Trade Union Confederations to be acceptable. It was afraid of Communist Party control of the Unions, and sought to by-pass this by being able to start another Confederation.

The Communist Party and all the rest of the left opposed the division of the Trade Union Movement into more than one Confederation (as we in Britain would strongly oppose it here). After much heated argument, the Government decided that only one Confederation could be recognised.

The Socialist Party policy on this was well known, and was confirmed to us from a number of sources, including Socialist Party members.

On 7th February, there was the first demonstration by the alternative left, a very big one called by the Workers' Committees of Lisbon, and coinciding with NATO manoeuvres off the coast of Portugal.

This demonstration was forbidden by the government, and opposed by all three parties in it, the People's Democratic Party (PPD) (right wing), the Socialist Party (PS), and the Communist Party (PCP). They all spoke out against the demonstration, especially the Communist Party.

It became a turning point for the Armed Forces Movement (MFA). The soldiers were in the streets to defend the American Embassy, but the demonstrators spoke to them, and the soldiers allowed the demonstration to pass the Embassy on condition that they did not damage it. This was done, with perfect self-discipline by the marchers. When the demo arrived at the Ministry of Labour, the soldiers actually joined it.

Spinola had had the idea of making Copcon (the Home Secretary Forces) into a repressive force, but this meant that the Copcon soldiers were constantly in touch with the workers, and were influenced by them, so it completely misfired and made it the most progressive force rather than a repressive one.

On 14th August, we attended a Socialist Party demonstration. We observed that the crowd was composed almost entirely of strikingly prosperous looking people. In Portugal, social class difference is much easier to see than in Britain, because it is a country of much greater contrasts. Yet even in Britain, let alone Portugal, this would have been a surprising crowd to see on a Labour/Trade Union march, it was not composed of people one would expect to see on marches at all. It was also very much a middle-aged crowd, with very few young people.

Some of us watched it separately, and we independently noticed that every single slogan (except a very brief chant of "PS") was negative, shouting their opposition to the Prime Minister especially (Vasco Goncalves), and also to the Copcon (some officers of which had recently issued a statement in reply to that of the so-called "moderate" officers).

I cannot recollect ever before being at a Rally with entirely negative slogans. (And there was a lot of slogan shouting — it is very much the thing on Portuguese demonstrations).

I put these points to a personal assistant of Mario Soares, who said that it was a very poor and small demonstration, because people were now tired of marches and demonstrations.

Also on 14th August, we later went to a Communist Party rally. This was an indoor meeting, which was already full and proceeding, and there was quite a large overflow outside with which we mingled, listening to the loudspeaker relay. The speech expressed the need for anti-fascist unity. It complained that the Socialist Party appeared to condone the violent attacks on PCP headquarters in the North, or at least did not unite against them. It made points on this which seemed perfectly proper and reasonable. However, it did not seem to have any points going beyond the call for anti-fascist unity. To me, this seemed inadequate. The crowd was quite different from the PS, mixed ages, mixed social classes, many workers.

In the British press afterwards these two rallies were portrayed as a "confrontation". There was supposed to be great tension between them, with the authorities trying in vain to avoid this "confrontation". This was arrant nonsense. They were two events by opposing organisations which were held on the same day in the same city but were a long way apart and in no sense was there a tense confrontation.

On 20th August, in Lisbon, we attended the most marvellous demonstration I have ever seen and participated in. It was called by the Workers' Committees and Neighbourhood Committees in the Lisbon area, and was very large. It was called to support the document issued by some of the Copcon officers, against the "moderate" document by the nine so-called "moderate" officers. It also marched under such slogans as these:

An end to the poverty of the peasants.
Long live the peasants, brothers of the workers,
Workers and peasants, soldiers and sailors, united we will win.
Against fascism, against capitalism, for the popular offensive.
Against *imperialisms,* for national independence.

and several others.

There were shipyard workers and soldiers – the most unmilitary looking soldiers you could possible imagine – banner upon banner – surprisingly large numbers of women – people with their children – from factories and neighbourhoods, all kinds of industries – agricultural workers – sailors – thousands of people, taking over the streets of Lisbon, absolutely peacefully. And no policemen – at least, we saw four (one of them sitting in an abandoned tram), except when we passed the police station when we saw a couple of dozen (yes, we marched with it). Trams and buses were just left where they stuck, in many cases. Lots of spectators, as well as all the marchers − and many of them joining in with the slogans and waving. I saw a bus driver waving both arms and joining in with the slogans, then he remembered his bus was still moving, ever so slowly but moving, and he grabbed the steering wheel.

It was completely self-disciplined, self-stewarded. I thought of all the people in Britain who thought of Portugal as a fearful place to be at this time, because of press reports, and then looked at the reality of being inside the Portuguese revolution and feeling the intoxicating sense of freedom, the mixture of determination and jubilation, all these thousands of people expressing their desire for socialism and democracy in a country so recently emerging from fascism and fear. How lucky to be in Portugal on 20th August 1975 sharing this experience!

Violence in the north

We visited Aveiro, which lies about 160 miles north of Lisbon and 40 miles south of Oporto. It was the first place where the PCP headquarters was attacked. This occurred on 18th July. Mario Soares leader of the PS, had spoken at Oporto on 17th July. The theme had been: against the MFA, against the PCP, against Vasco Goncalves. There had also earlier been an inflammatory speech by the Bishop of Aveiro. He had spoken against the takeover by the workers of the church Radio Station in Lisbon, and the takeover by the workers of *Republica*, but these initiatives were not led by the PCP anyway.

The first pattern of attacks on PC headquarters was that advantage would be taken of a fair or market or some other cause of crowds. Rightwing agitators would move in to get people excited, shouting anti-communist slogans and generally stirring up trouble. They often accused the communists of being the new PIDE (secret police). The core seemed to be the same group of people moving from place to place, but undoubtedly other people did join in from the street throwing stones, etc. There were never two attacks on different places simultaneously, so it appeared that the hardcore was not big enough to stage more than one attack at a time.

In Aveiro, all the windows of the PCP HQs had been smashed and it must have been quite frightening to be inside at the time, but the form of the attacks was relatively simple, stones and the like – not bombs.

It left a good deal of bitterness, because although the

army was very slow to come to its defence, they did so in the end, reacting to the extent of firing shots over the heads of the crowd. Unfortunately one weapon misfired and killed one of the soldiers.

An unfounded rumour was put round the next day that the soldier had been shot because he refused to defend communists.

The pattern of the attacks however had changed by the time we visited Aveiro, partly because they started to meet resistance from inside the attacked premises. They now use groups coming in cars and throwing incendiaries, and people on the streets are relucant to take part in this kind of attack. The very latest kind of attack is different again – an aeroplane is now being used to drop incendiaries on forests. With the dry hot weather, of course, it is very easy to start extensive fires and an area which we passed through, and which was then quite peaceful, was in flames a few days later because of such an attack. At one and the same time this is a dangerous escalation of violence and can do enormous damage, and it is also an expression of the weakness of the fascists. This kind of attack using technology is very different from mass demonstrations.

However there is no doubt that quite large sections of the population in the north are prepared at least to tolerate, when not actively supporting, anti communist attacks. Another example of a different kind of attack in a smaller place was of a village with about 10,000 population only about 20 of whom were members of the PCP. A mob of people went to the house of one member and took everything out into the street. This was one of the rare daylight attacks and the local people only recognised about 6 of the attackers, the rest coming from outside the village.

In Agueda the PCP centre was attacked in daylight and 52 people were identified of whom only 13 were workers. The remainder were owners of carsale rooms, landowners, small industrialists and people who had been "cleansed", i.e. fascists.

Why should this kind of thing happen in the Aveiro district and in the North of Portugal generally, whereas it is not happening in the South? Aveiro itself is a relatively prosperous district. There is some industry, though it is relatively new and industrial class consciousness is not well developed except in a few sections. Many of the workers are also peasants as well, working their land when they finish in the factory. They work very hard but achieve a relatively good standard of living. There is also a considerable amount of emigration to the USA, and the anti-communism is particularly anti-Cuba, because the Portuguese emigrant workers have been influenced by the anti-Cuba propaganda in the USA. There is also a very strong campaign to persuade the many ill-educated poor people that Russia is a very sinister place indeed where people get an injection behind the ear when over 60 to kill them off, the children are taken away from parents and that everybody dresses alike. In the north generally there are many very small peasants, unlike the Alentejo where most of the agricultural workers are wage earners. These small peasants have been frightened by tales of their land would be taken away from them. They have probably gained the least from the revolution, and are often very much in the hands of intermediaries who sell their products and greatly fear the development of co-operatives.

The north is therefore quite deeply conservative and is fertile land for the rightwing. The communists were harrassed even in the election campaign, with cars being destroyed, and so on.

Despite this, and despite the attack on the PCP headquarters, I noticed that when we were in Aveiro, it was possible for us to have a lengthy discussion in a restaurant with the district secretary of the PCP in a completely open manner. The discussion was conspicuous being translated back and forth Portuguese into English, and at times quite heated because we disagreed with him on quite a lot of matters. It was also lengthy (three hours!) Yet there was not so much as a nasty remark sent in our direction, though a number of people were quite clearly listening. Even though this was the north of Portugal which is portrayed in such a sinister light, and where anti-communism is more prevalent than anywhere else in Portugal there was a good deal less fear and risk in discussing communism with a communist than there would be for example discussing the Irish question with Irish people in many parts of Britain.

The political pattern of attack has also been changing. The local PS is quite small, left wing, and has reasonably cordial relations with the local PCP. It is certainly not violently anti-communist. However it does transmit the statements issued nationally by the PS. Following the speech by Mario Soares on 17th July in Oporto, there was a big PS meeting on 25th July in Saint Joao da Madeira addressed by Manuel Alegre and Salgado Zenha, both members of the national secretariat of the PS. Zenha was Minister of Justice in the first three governments and is the right hand man of Mario Soares. Slogans were; death to the communists; Cunhal is provoking unemployment; Cunhal is responsible for economic chaos. In this particular place the local top PS leader took the lead in an attack on CP headquarters but he had been a prominent member of Caetano's party under fascism. The PS there issued a statement saying they could not be responsible for the physical safety of PCP members or their children.

However, now that the PS has been successfully used as a cover in the initial stages of these attacks the reaction is now coming out much more openly and clearly, mainly in the form of the PPD. This is openly belligerent. When the Aveiro attack took place the PPD published a statement which did not exactly support the violence but certainly condoned it, saying that it proved that the people were not scared of the PCP and could take justice into their own hands.

The anti PCP attacks seem to have been quite carefully planned, with carefully chosen dates and places, and good organisation. There is a so called army of liberation (ELP) being organised in Spain, and there is open talk in north Portugal that there are clandestine cells of the ELP in being.

The attitude of the leadership of the PS gave the reaction cover in the beginning. Now the PS is quieter, and there has been some division in its ranks. The PPD has come out more openly.

Political groups and parties

There is a multiplicity of political groupings in Portugal now, all taking full advantage of the freedom of expression which exists. We brought home many papers published by these groups and parties, and talked to members of several of them.

Together the left groupings outside the PS and PCP have a considerable following now and are gaining strength in the unions.

As an example of one of these groups here is a short account of a discussion with one of them, the movement for left socialism (MES) which started in 1969, got stronger, but was not well organised up to 25th April. It thinks that the anti-fascist fight cannot be separated from the anti-capitalist fight. At 25th April it was concentrated in Lisbon, but is now nationwide and is strong amongst metal workers and textile workers.

It considers that the PS is social democratic, which it defines as being not for an end to capitalism but just for changes in it. It thinks the PCP is a party of the workers and the left but does not think that its strategy leads to socialism but rather to state capitalism.

It is concentrating its organising efforts on workers, peasants, and the armed forces. It has a weekly paper, *Poder Popular* (Popular Power).

It favours the development of direct democracy which first started as a spontaneous development among workers in the form of workers' committees and neighbourhood committees, then was adopted by some of the left groups including MES and LUAR (League for Unity and Revolutionary Action) then was adopted by the General Assembly of the Armed Forces Movement (MFA).

Mes considers that the two processes which have been happening since 25th April are alternatives and that if one triumphs the other will fail. One process is the development of the Constituent Assembly, composed of various political parties. The other is the development of a structure which starts at Workers' Committees and Neighbourhood Committees which are based on Popular. Assemblies of all the people in the works or neighbourhood. The Popular Assemblies elect the Committees which deal with their relevant problems as far as this can be done at local level. They also then form the basis of District Popular Assemblies, Regional Popular Assemblies and a National Popular Assembly.

Mes considers that in voting in elections for a Constituent Assembly or Parliament, people can easily vote against their real interests, even voting fascist or capitalist. On the other hand of course, they can well vote for a socialist programme. However the programmes and what the Parties say at election times can be very different from the policies which they actually operate when they gain power, and because the whole process is considerably removed from the daily life of the ordinary people, the parties control the process and the people, instead of the people controlling the parties.

Mes considers that "Popular Power" (direct democracy) cannot be controlled in this way by parties who desert their programmes, because people involved in each stage are electing on the basis of the problems which they themselves are familiar with in their workplace or neighbourhood. They are in the much better position to evaluate the actions of those elected than in the more remote Parliamentary process. Then at the District or higher levels, again those involved in the elections are able to base their judgement on much more first-hand and detailed knowledge of the actual performance of candidates.

Mes considers that there is no place for social democracy in Portugal because the capitalist crisis is so deep. There are only two alternatives — return to fascism or on to socialism. It is impossible to get conciliation of classes in Portugal because there is no economic basis on which it could be based.

Appendix:
strategic programme
of the armed forces movement

Adopted by the General Assembly of the Armed Forces'
Movement (MFA) on the 8th July 1975.

Introduction

The alliance of the people and the MFA has been a constant
feature of the revolutionary process right up to the present
moment. The act of liberation undertaken on the 25th April, fol-
lowed by a rapid development in the outlook of the MFA and the
progressive political parties, together with the implementation of
measures of a political and economic character, has facilitated
cohesion between the people and the MFA.

Meanwhile, maintenance and consolidation of the alliance between the people and the MFA, has to develop towards satisfying
the deepest aspirations of the exploited classes. From this point
of view it was urgent to continue the work that was begun on the
25th April 1974. It is within the framework of a cultural revolution, in the application of the military and civilian potentialities
that exist, in the technical field and in the field of human and
material relations, that the people will be mobilised decisively
for the revolution.

Furthermore practice has begun to confirm this analysis which
is evident in other ways. This fundamental premise for the consolidation of the alliance, depends upon the creation of conditions such that the twin engine of the Portuguese revolution is
maintained and made more powerful. To mobilise the people
for the revolution, it is necessary that the working masses should
be assured of active participation, which means forms of popular organisations, in democratic independent tasks and co-
operation in each basic unit.

It is necessary to use this fundamental reality — the alliance of
the people and the MFA — in a concrete way stimulating, supporting it, for the defence and the dynamisation of the revolution
that is taking place. The defence and the dynamisation of the

revolution, in the phase that we are now in, involves realising the following tasks:

a. encouraging revolutionary participation on the part of the masses, that is to say creating and developing unit groupings with the perspective of stimulating genuine organs of popular power.

b. defending the revolution against the attacks of reactionary forces by making people profoundly conscious of the needs of the process and the creation of defensive organisms.

c. winning the battle for the economy. As long as production is insufficient for the overall necessities of the country, the working masses need to make a great effort. It is fundamental therefore to win the battle for the economy by overcoming the weak development of the productive forces, by amplifying and developing workers' control, by enlarging the state sector and by seeking the accumulation that is necessary to our economic independence.

To realise the points indicated above it is necessary:

In the Field of Internal Politics

a. to create and develop a large state sector which should reflect domination of the national economy by a democratic state as opposed to a private economy dominated by monopoly capital which paralyses the development of production.

b. to replace an agrarian structure which has deep feudal roots by another which makes possible progressive expansion, an objective clearly defined by agrarian reform, and the application of which must be scrupulously controlled by the organised working masses of the countryside.

c to clean up the state apparatus and to decentralise it so as to build a new apparatus that is popularly based, so that through effective coordination, the potentialities for initiative on the part of local popular organs of power are dynamised, linked in such a way that they enjoy large autonomy in decision-making and are in a position to act as a countervailing force in the domain of financial power, thereby putting the national product of labour effectively in the hands of the working masses.

d. to encourage and support forms of control of the means of production by the workers.

e. to define an overall economic policy in which are pin-pointed the priority sectors for development.

f. to define an economic policy for each of these sectors.

External Politics

a. to guarantee to its ultimate conclusion the accomplishment of decolonisation in Africa since, looking at the matter clearly and without passion from the standpoint of history, the independent future of Portugal must be based upon fraternal relations with our ex-colonies in the political, social and economic fields.

b. to avoid every kind of ideological political or economic hegemony over the Portuguese revolutionary process; to guarantee the maintainance of cordial relations with all peoples of the world; to consolidate an economic power that guarantees national independence.

We do not intend either to ignore parties dedicated to the construction of socialism nor to militarise the people. We mean to create a mass organisation which, at this moment of time, within a proper outlook on the class struggle, brings together unit by unit the workers and takes in hand specific tasks for the defence of the revolution, as defined above.

We assert quite specifically that defence of the revolution requires consolidation of the conquests that have been won through organisation, vigilance, work, discipline and authority and with the effective advance in the rooting of political power in the hands of the working masses. This mass organisation — promoting by its formation, by its practical experience, the unity of the working masses — will create conditions for political parties interested in the construction of socialism to find forms of cooperation and understanding that lead to the direction of these efforts towards a suitable consolidation of the political advance guard in the revolutionary process.

These objectives can be achieved by realising the programme of political action adopted by the Revolutionary Council, by the provisional government acting in a unified way, by a policy of moulding events to help the revolutionary process, and by the practice on the part of the MFA of exemplary unity, of austerity, of authority and discipline. This means revolutionary practice, criticism and self-criticism in the heart of the MFA. In the light of what we have said above, we suggest, in what follows, the structure of alliance between the people and the MFA.

Explanation of the organic structure

a. the structure of the alliance, People-MFA, will have three fundamental lines: that of the AFM, that of the people, and that of the Government. In this phase of transition, the state apparatus ought to be cleaned up and progressively replaced, its powers (administrative and financial) decentralised, encouraging local initiative and the progressive assumption of power by popular organisms.

b. committees of people who live in a neighbourhood, committees of workers and every other organisation that is popularly based will form popular assemblies locally for parishes and for zones that are yet to be defined.

c. starting with these local assemblies municipal assemblies will be formed, and so on stage by stage up to a popular national assembly.

d. participation on the part of the MFA begins in the municipal assemblies and district assemblies through ADUs (assemblies of delegates from units); in the regional assemblies through ADRs (assemblies of delegates from regiments), and in the national assembly through the assembly of the MFA. This means that the ADU are assemblies of units – from the Army, from the Navy, from the Air Force and from the Security Forces.

e. the Revolutionary Council is the supreme organ of national sovereignty.

f. the popular assemblies are supported by the MFA and every other organ of the state apparatus exercising over these an administrative control on the part of the public in which they participate.

Starting Popular Organisations

a. In the first phase, the ADU will encourage, with meetings to convey information and clarify ideas, the development of neighbourhood committees and committees of workers where these do not already exist. Where some such structures already do exist, meetings will also take place to convey information about the true objectives of the MFA. Following that, through contact with organisations at the base, experience of what has actually happened will be collected and made available to improve procedures and to get better results. When the MFA has sized up the situation in this way, recognition will be given to these organisations.

b. In a second phase shortly afterwards, the formation of popular assemblies, locally and on a borough basis will be encouraged.

c. In a third phase after a somewhat longer lapse of time, the formation of district popular assemblies will be encouraged.

d. In a fourth, long-term phase, the formation of regional popular assemblies will be encouraged.

e. The national popular assembly, a highest organ of popular participation, will be the last and most distant stage in this structure.

Statutory Norms

General

The popular organisation proposed is fundamentally constituted by the committees of workers and the neighbourhood committees. We also regard a basic organisms the village councils, cooperatives, associations of small and middle-sized farmers, collectives and every other association of the people. Structures that are being started as a result of various initiatives ought to be linked to well-defined organisms at the base — neighbourhood committees, workers' committees — which will be extended so as to absorb and to regulate expressions of the people's will and to consolidate and guarantee the revolutionary process as far as tasks of organisations at the base is concerned.

Finally, neighbourhood meetings and workers' meetings and other organisations at the base will undertake tasks of defending the revolution. The present statutory norms relate to those already existing in the various organisations that need to be extended so as to include the objectives here defined.

Principles of Orientation in Popular Organisation

Objectives: the fundamental and ultimate objective is to construct the socialist society defined by the political plan of action of the revolutionary council. As this objective can only be attained with unity, all levels of popular organisation must and can be based on unity.

This concept of unity is defined as follows:

- independence as regards parties;
- democratic representation starting with the neighbourhood committees or production units;
- association to resolve specific problems.

The best guarantee for obtaining this objective is that the MFA, a movement that is above parties, accompanies and encourages the process by supporting, by integrating and by recognising the organisations which make good the pursuit of this objective in practice.

Tasks of organisations at the base:

Workers' committees, neighbourhood committees etc. will have in addition to specific functions, to promote — in accordance with these characteristics — the following activities:

- political work by means of information and clarification in professional sectors or zones of high population density;
- social action in the field of health and assistance, culture and sport, illiteracy, housing and town-planning, transport etc.;
- economic action in the battle for the economy, control over the means of production in the nationalised and private sectors, supplies and prices, etc.;
- vigilance, in defence of installations and urban areas by means of physical presence everywhere, control of entry, the channelling of information to the official organs concerned etc. In special cases (strategically important points in the national economy), on the initiative of the MFA and under its control, the framework may take the form of tasks of self defence;
- reinforcement of the People-MFA alliance as an activity always present in these organizations.

Tasks of Popular Assemblies:

The popular assemblies have the following fundamental purposes to serve:

- transmission up to the appropriate level of aspirations, opinions and needs of the populations they represent;

- involvement in local, regional and national planning through competent organs acting as agents of the people concerned;
- dealing with the revenues and control over the activity of administrative organs and their readiness to respond to the needs of the people;
- setting up in the local organs of popular power a people's tribunal to resolve problems which are not of a criminal character;

The Process of Formation:

a. the committee of popular organisations is elected at plenary meetings, voting by raised hands;
b. in the organisations at the base, elected members are recallable by the plenary assemblies which elected them;
c. in the popular assemblies, elected members are recallable by the assemblies themselves;

Concerning the Constitution

a. organisations at the base (neighbourhood meetings, workers' meetings etc.) will have their present constitutions extended in such a manner as to fulfil the tasks already defined.
b. local popular assemblies:
    - delegates of the organisation at the base;
    - delegates of local authorities
c. municipal popular assemblies:
    - delegates from the ADUs;
    - delegates of the APLs;
    - delegates of authorities and governments bodies;
d. District popular assemblies:
    - delegates of the ADUs (including unit commanders);
    - delegates of the local authorities and governmental bodies;
    - delegates of trade union organisations.
e. Regional popular assemblies:
    - delegates of Assemblies of regimental delegates (ADR), who include commanders of military regions;
    - delegates of popular district assemblies (APD);
    - delegates of local authorities and government bodies;
    - delegates of trade union organisations.
f. The national popular assembly:
    - still to be defined.

Functioning

a. Decisions in all these organisations will be taken by voting with raised hands.
b. representatives of local authorities, of government bodies (regional planning offices, regional agrarian institutions etc) and delegates of trade union bodies will have equal rights as regards presentation of proposals, votes and expressions of views.
c. decisions taken in assembly bind all components of the structure to carry them out.

Final Provisions

1. The present norms do not have a rigid character and in applying them account should be taken of specific local characteristics and the way things can most vigorously develop.
2. This statement should be considered as a document for guidance in the practical undertakings of military units and popular organisms. The structure corresponding to the present state of development in popular organisation only goes as far as local popular assemblies. This phase needs to be duly consolidated and it will be through the dynamic of the revolutionary process itself that the possibility of advance to the higher forms of organisation will come about.

Printed in Great Britain
by Amazon